Python:

Learn the Easiest Program Coding for the Absolute Beginner

Jon Stinkster

ISBN-13: 978-1540399045
ISBN-10: 1540399044

CONTENTS

INTRODUCTION

Congratulations on purchasing Python: Learn the Easiest Program Coding for the Absolute Beginner and thank you for doing so.

The following chapters will discuss how to get started with Python and why it is the best option for you, even if you are just getting started with program as a very beginner. Python is a simple programming language, one that is based on the English language and has gotten rid of a lot of the clutter and mess that plagues some of the other great programming languages. While it may not have some of the design features and speed that some of the other languages have, it is easy to read, can combine with other programs, and is really a fantastic place for the beginner to get started.

This guidebook is going to discuss some of the different aspects of Python and will give you plenty of opportunities to practice using different codes within Python. We will discuss why you should choose the Python program over some of the other options, some of the steps that you should take in order to get the program downloaded on your computer (and it is free!), and then the basic commands that you can learn in order to get started on your very first code.

If all of this sounds intimidating, don't worry. Python is an easy language to learn and for the most part, you will simply need a few statements in order to get something to print up on your screen. We will walk you through the steps that you need to create statements, comment, operands, variables, and everything else that you need to get started with coding in Python.

Now is the time to jump in and really get your feet wet with the great Python language. It is simple to use even for the beginner, but has enough power and great features that you would be amazed at how much you are able to do with Python as you progress. Take a look through this guidebook and learn exactly how Python works and how you can make the codes that you want, even as a beginner with this amazing product.

There are plenty of books on this subject on the market, thanks again for choosing this one! Every effort was made to ensure it is full of as much useful information as possible, please enjoy!

The Basics of Getting Started with Python

When you are working in the computer world, there are all sorts of people you will run across. There are those who have just gotten started with learning about programming and how a computer works all the way up to those who have been working with computers for years and who can write some impressive codes in the process. While the professionals can make coding look like a breeze, those who are beginners may be scared away by the complicated statements, how messy some of the lines can look, and they may just give up assuming that it is too hard for them.

There are a number of different programming languages that you can use. They will vary on their complications as well as how powerful they are for what you want to create. Many of these are really popular for experienced programmers, such as Java and C++, but they are really confusing for someone who has just gotten started with programming for themselves.

If you have ever gotten started with programming and just felt that you couldn't read what was written or just couldn't figure out how to write the code that you wanted, Python may be the right answer for you. Python is one of the easiest programming languages to use. It is based off the ABC system in English, so there won't be a ton of words and phrases that you won't understand. It was also written with simplicity in mind so there aren't a bunch of lines, brackets, and other figures that jumble up the code and make it hard to read.

How Python got started

Python got started in 1989 by Guido van Rossum. Van Rossum started out in programming as more of a hobby. During this time, van Rossum had been working with the Dutch CWI research institute, but this project was terminated before it was completed. Using the knowledge, he had learned from this project, van Rossum created a new language, commonly referred to as the ABC language, which is now the basis of the Python programming language.

The ABC language makes Python so easy to use. You can extend on it and add more complexity and power to your codes if needed, but at the core, this is a basic programming language that even beginners are able to use. Since the language is easy to use and has all the power that you want from other programming languages, it didn't take long before Python became really popular.

Over time, van Rossum did work to add some new updates to Python to make it even easier to use. But some worried about what would happen with Python if something happened to van Rossum. Because of this concern, van Rossum allowed the language to become open sourced. This means that others can develop and update Python, allowing the program to go into the future and become even better.

Thanks to this open sourcing, there have now been several new versions of Python that have some great features. Python 2.0 was first released in 2000 and in 2008 Python 3 became available as well. Most programmers still use Python 2 because of its ease to use and its backwards compatibility that is not available in Python 3.

Because Python is now open sourced, there are even more updates that are coming out that makes it perfect for everyone to use. There are two current types of Python that are being used, though it is possible that others could be made at the same time as well. Python 2.0 and Python 3.0 are the main types that you can use and many beginners may be curious as to which one they should try out. Honestly, it is more about preference and what you would like to do with the program as both are great options.

Python 2

Python 2 was released during 2000 and had a few changes made to it. This version has a really transparent development process that allows the user to feel comfortable with using it in their lives. It is also more oriented on the community so that others can make changes and leave comments to help out others. This one is the most common that programmers will use since it has been around for longer and since Python 3.0 is not backwards compatible so you are not able to use your codes from the original on the new one.

Python 3

Python 3 is another great choice that you can make when it comes to picking out your Python programming. This version was first released during 2008. Unlike some other versions of2.0, this is not an update to the system, but rather a complete change to it. There are some great features that add more power and if you want to get the most out of using Python, this would be a good choice to choose.

Keep in mind that you are not going to be able to use the backwards compatibility between the two versions of Python. But Python 3 does have the benefit of a coder that will mark out the places that you need to make changes between the two programs to keep things easier for you when converting.

Overall, while Python 2 is still the most widely used of the Python programs, it is anticipated that it won't be long before Python 3 becomes the one that most programmers are using.

The Benefits of Python

There are so many features that you are going to enjoy about Python, especially if you are new to programming and feel a bit nervous about seeing how it will work for you. Some of the best features that you will enjoy include:

- A style and syntax that is really simple so that even the beginner is able to read through it.

- Language that is really easy to use. You will be able to write out the code without dealing with bugs or complicated syntaxes that can confuse you and cause a mess.

- Python contains a big library to help you get the code started. This can save you time and effort.

- Python has the ability to work with other programming tasks. This makes it easier to connect with other web servers, doing searches or texts, and even changing files.

- This language is easy to work with other options. If you want to expand out to other languages, such as C++ or C, it is easy to do. This allows you more options working with the program so you can get all the ease along with all the power in one.

- Python is an interactive language. You are able to add in the IDLE development environment so that it is easy to write out your codes and test it to see what will work. This allows you to experiment and see what will work as you learn.

- The Python language can be used on any unit that you want including Mac OS X, Windows, Unix, and Linux.

- The Python language is free. It has become open sourced so that anyone is able to use it and make changes if needed. This makes sure that it is always able to expand while you get a great product for free.

- While Python is a simple language to learn, it has advanced features that you can learn to use such as generators and comprehensions.

- If you perform an error, it is easy to catch these quickly. If you mix together types that don't go together, you will be able to see the errors right away and make the adjustments.

- Python includes a wide variety of data types that you will be able to use in your codes including strings, lists, numbers, and dictionaries.

Even though Python is a really simple programming language to work with, it is one of the best that you can choose. You are going to love that the language is easy to read, that it allows you to experiment and catch errors early on, and that it still has a lot of the power that you are used to with some of the other languages. All of these things come together to provide you with a fantastic programming language to learn.

Why should I choose Python?

There are so many programming languages that you can choose from. Some are great for beginners and will help you to get comfortable in programming while others are really powerful and can give you so many options when it comes to the strength of your codes and what you are able to do. With all these options to go with, you may be wondering why you should choose Python over one of the other languages.

Python is considered one of the best languages for beginners. It is easy to read and learn and you won't get too confused in the process. Some of the other benefits of choosing Python over one of your other options includes:

Readability

When it comes to finding a language that is really easy to read, Python is one of the best. Other programming languages are really hard to read through, adding in a lot of brackets and words that may not even be English. You may read through them and find that you are confused in no time. But when it comes to Python, even beginners will be able to read through it in no time. You simply need to understand what some of the keywords mean and you are on the right track to being able to read through and create your own code.

Large libraries

Since Python has been around for more than 25 years, it has many codes that have been written into the system. Especially since it has become open sourced, it is easier than ever to go into the library and find some of the libraries that you need to help you write your code. You can use this to finish off the program you are working on or if you need to create something new. You can visit the library and see all of the codes that are already present. This can help to speed up the process so that you can insert your special statements and have the code be written for you.

For a beginner, having a large library in your programming language can be helpful. You should take some time to look through this library and see which codes are already available to you through Python. This can help you to learn how some of the codes work and even speeds up the process because you can just click and select some of the codes that you want to use rather than just writing them all out.

Community

When it comes to online communities, Python has one of the best. There are even conferences as well as many local and national networking opportunities that you can enjoy. If you are able to go to one of these, there are so many things that you can learn about from others who have used the program. Or you can go online and connect with others, ask questions, and learn as much about the Python program as possible.

When you first get started with programming, the community may not seem that important. You may figure that you are doing the coding on your own, so why would you need a community to help. But you never know when you may have a questions, may get stuck on something, or just need some basic help You can use the online communities to look up or ask the questions that you need ahead of time. Plus, it is always nice to meet other people who may have the same love of programming as you.

Easy to test out

Python allows you to install the interpreter and try out your codes right away. You can try out the parts as you write them out to determine how they will show up on the screen and to catch issues right when they happen. Plus, when you are all done, it can be nice to take a look at the program and see how it is going to work. For beginners, it can be nice to experiment a bit with some new codes and check them out right away to see if the code was written correctly or to see if it looks good on the computer.

Works with other programs

The nice thing about using Python is you are able to combine it with some of the other programming languages to make it more powerful. You will still get some of the simplicity of using Python, but you can add in some more power when you combine with Java or C++. It is going to take some time to work on transferring the information, but it can really expand what you are doing with your new code when you can combine them.

In the beginning, you are probably going to focus on just writing your codes and getting familiar with the Python code and how it will work in your life. This is enough for a beginner. But as you gain some more confidence and get used to the Python programming, you may find that there are some other things that you want to do that just aren't possible without some help. The fact that Python will work with some of the other programing languages make sit perfect for expanding what you are able to do after gaining some experience.

There are a lot of great benefits that come with using Python, but it is important to remember that there are some things that may not work the way that you want. Some of the issues that you may run into when working with the Python language include:

1. Speed is a bit slow—the speed that you find with Python may be a bit slower than other languages. Now, if you've never used another programming language, you probably won't notice this speed difference. But for those who have done some work on other platforms, the speed could be a bit of an annoyance.

2. Doesn't work on mobile phones—right now the Python language doesn't work with mobile phones. This can be a problem if you are trying to write a code that works just for phones or one that you want to work with computers as well as phones. But since Python is open sourced, it may be something that programmers will be able to develop later on.

3. Design restrictions—there are going to be some restrictions that come with the design elements of Python. Since it is a simple language, sometimes you won't be able to do as much with the design as you can with some of the other programming languages. You can combine it with some of the other languages to help with this a bit, but you should be aware that the design my not meet up with some of your expectations.

For everyone who has wanted to get started in programming but felt that it would be too complicated for them or they worried that the codes they looked at were kind of a mess, Python is the best option to go with. It is designed to go off the English language, looks nice when written out, and with the large library, you are sure to find many of the codes that you need right inside the program to save you some time. With a bit of practice with Python, you will find that getting your program started is easier than you would imagine.

Setting Up Python on Your Computer

As we have discussed, Python is a fantastic language to use when you want to get into programming. Whether you are just getting started with programming for the first time or you have been working in this field for some time, Python has some great benefits that will really help you create awesome code. But before you are able to start writing your codes, you will need to download Python, as well as the required add-ons, to make sure that this software program properly.

Python is able to work on many different types of computers. For those who have Ubuntu and Mac computers, Python is already installed on your computer. This helps you to get started faster as you will just need to find the Python icon and then get started.

The ability of Python to work on many different types of computer systems without having to worry about crashing or other issues is one of the reasons that Python is so popular. You are able to use it on Mac, Windows, Linux, and more without an issue and some of these systems already have Python installed on them. This saves you so much time and hassle and can make using Python even easier than before.

Python does work on Windows computers as well, but you will need to go through and install Python onto the system. The program is free so you won't have to worry about any extra fees to get the language to work, you will just need to find the right downloader and get it sent to your computer. For Windows 7 to Windows 10, here are the steps for downloading Python to your computer:

- Download the program—you will be able to choose between Python 2 and Python 3 depending on your needs. They do things a bit differently so look up the differences and see which one is going to help you the most. Many programmers still use Python 2.

- Click the Installer—when you are ready to download, the Python Installer will come up. You should choose to do a customized installation.

- A box is going to pop up and you should take the time to click all of the boxes that are available with original features and then click on continue.

- Once the program has gotten this far and started downloading, you can open up the Control Panel and look up Environment.

- Now go to the System Environment Variable, click on the Edit button, and then click on your Environment Variables.

- Click on User Variables. You can either edit one that is already there or create one that was brand new.

  o If you want to create a new path, you can select PATH as the new name and then add it to your directories. Make sure that you separate out the variable values using a semicolon.

  o If you choose to edit a path that is already there, you should make sure that you place all the values on different lines. Click on the New button and then place the directories on different lines.

- You can now open up the command prompt under the start button.

- When this opens, type in Python so that you can load your Python interpreter. You can type in Exit and then hit the Enter button so that the command prompt comes up.

Picking a text editor

When you are working on Python, you will need to install a text editor of some kind. The program will not be able to read through your code unless you have this in place. If you plan to use a Windows computer, the Notepad is going to work just fine and it is already on your computer so doesn't take much time to get it all done. You do need to be careful and choose Notepad rather than Word; Word is not an editor and it will not work in this function with Python so don't get the two confused.

If you are looking to install Notepad on your computer, Notepad++ is a great option to use for Windows. For other computers, text wrangler is a great option. You can choose whichever ones you would like so take a look at the different options that are available and choose the one that will meet your needs the best for writing the code. When you are ready to set up the text editor on your computer, use the following steps:

Windows

- Download and install Notepad ++ if you don't already have this on your computer.

- Go into Notepad ++ and open the settings up. Click on your Language Menu and then the Tab Settings.

- Click the box next to Expand Tabs

- Check to see if the value is 4

- Click again to close

Now it is set up to work as a text editor with Python when you are ready to get started.

Mac

- Download and install Text Wrangler or another text editor of your choice.

- It will ask you to register, but this is not required. Just click on Cancel for registering if the box comes up.

- Follow the instructions that come up so that you can get the editor ready to go.

Don't forget about IDLE

In most cases, your Python download is going to come with IDLE, but make sure to check before you get too far. IDLE stands for Integrated Development and Learning Environment. This is basically the environment that you will work within when you are with Python. Python basically is not going to work if you don't have IDLE around to provide the environment to write the code and make it show up on the computer.

If you don't like IDLE, it is possible for you to pick out a different environment if you would like. IDLE is one of the best to do with Python and can provide you with a lot of great benefits. Since it already comes with Python, it is going to be free, which is better than what you will find with other options. But you must make sure that you have some kind of environment in place to help the Python program to work.

Installing Python on your computer is really easy. You won't have to worry about paying a big fee to work on this program and the installation really only takes a short amount of time. With a couple clicks on your computer and ensuring that you have the proper environment and text editor in place, you will be able to get started with writing some amazing code!

Some of the Basics You Should Know to Get Started with Programming

Now that you have Python all set up on your computer, it is time to get to work and experiment with the program a little bit. While it is a simple program to learn in the beginning and you are going to be writing some fantastic codes in no time, you should still understand a bit about how the program works, what some of the different parts are all about, and how you can really get going. Let's spend some time looking at the different parts of Python programming so that you can write the codes you want.

Keywords

Any coding software that you use is going to have some keywords. These are words that will tell the interpreter what you want to happen in the code so they are important to know and understand. It is recommended that you don't use these anywhere else in your code to avoid confusion and error when the interpreter gets ahold of it since these are major action words. Some of the keywords that you should look at when working in the Python language include:

- False
- Finally
- Class
- Is
- Return
- Continue
- None
- For
- Try
- True

- Lambda

- Def

- Nonlocal

- From

- While

- Global

- Del

- And

- Not

- Raise

- In

- Except

- Break

- Pass

- Yield

- As

- If

- Elif

- Or

- Import

- Assert

- Else

- Import

This is a good list to keep on hand when you are writing your codes. This will help you to send the right information to the interpreter when you are writing through the code. Any time that you see an error message come up after writing out a code, make sure to check if you used one of those words properly within your statements.

Names of Identifiers

While working on a new code or program with Python, you will need to work with a few different things including variables, functions, entities, and classes. These will all have names that are also called identifiers. When you are creating the name of an identifier, regardless of the type you are working on, some of the rules that you should follow include:

- You should have letters, both lower case and upper case work well, the underscore symbol, and numbers. You are able to use any combination of these that you choose as well. Just make sure that there are no spaces inside.

- You can never start an identifier with a number. You are able to use something like sixdogs, but 6dogs would not be acceptable.

- The identifier should not be one of the keywords that were listed above and there should never be one of the keywords inside of it.

If you do go against one of these rules, you will notice that the program is going to close on you and a syntax error will occur. In addition to the rules above, you should ensure that the identifiers are easy to read with the human eye. This is important because while the identifier may follow the rules that were set out above, they can still have trouble when the human eye isn't able to understand what you are writing out.

When you are creating your identifier, make sure that you pick one that will be descriptive. Going with one that will describe what you the code is doing or what the variable contains is a good place to start. You should also be wary of using abbreviations because these aren't always understood by everyone and can cause some confusion.

Flow of the control

The flow of control is an important aspect of working in Python. You will want to write things out in the way that you want the interpreter to take a look at them. While every programming language is going to be a bit different, in Python you should write out the order of your statements in a list format. The computer and the interpreter will start with the very first command that is at the top of the list and then will work its way down to the last one.

So when you are writing out a new code and want to make sure that the interpreter understands what you want it to do, just write your commands out like you would a grocery list. You can then send your written code over to the interpreter and it will continue to read through everything, starting from the top, until it gets done.

This is a good way to make sure that the flow of control is as smooth as possible. You don't want to put commands right next to each other, but rather write them down in a list format. Start with the action that you want to happen first and then keep everything in order. The interpreter is not going to understand that you want it to skip around on some things to write it out like a list and keep everything in order.

If you are having some troubles getting the code to work out the way that you want, it may be time to take a look at the flow of control. Are you putting the steps in the wrong order for the list? Are you trying to combine a few steps or statements together that shouldn't be there? Take a look at your flow of control and determine if you need to move some things around to get it to all work out in the end.

Letter cases

Another thing that you should be aware of on the program is the letter case. Most of the other computer languages that you will work with treat lowercase and upper case letters the exact same, but they will actually mean different things in Python. This means that you will need to use them properly or you could end up with a mess when dealing with the execution. Also, all of the keywords that you are using in your code will be in lower case letters, except for the words True, False, and None.

When you are working on Python, you will want to keep a close eye on the different cases of the letters. You could run into an error simply because you have uppercase letters present when they should not be there. For the most part this won't be a huge issue, but still watch out for it to ensure that your code is going to turn out nicely.

Understanding some of these basics will make it easier for you to get your first code written with Python. Most people may be a bit scared to get started with a new programming language just because they assume that it will be too hard for them to master or they may have tried programming in the past and found it too confusion. But as you can see with some of these basics, Python is a language that anyone can learn, as long as you get some of the basics in place ahead of time. So now it is time to take a look at some of the things that you can really do with Python in order to start writing some codes and really understanding how this language works.

Comments, Statements, Variables, and Other Useful Commands in Python

There are really so many things that you are able to do with the Python programming language. While it may be one of the easiest programming languages to use, it has so many different functions and options that you are going to love to use. Here are a few examples of the different things that you can do on Python, including commands, variables, statements, and comments, that will help you to start writing code like a professional.

Comments

One of the first things that you should learn about when working on Python is comments. These are nice to know because you can insert them into your code in order to leave a note or tell the other person what they are supposed to do. For example, you may go into the Python library and pull out a code that will have comments beside each line. These comments can help you to know what the code is working on or what you are supposed to insert into each part in order to make the program work.

You can add as many comments to your code as you wish, but try not to go too overboard as this can start to make the code look bad. When you do the code right, the interpreter is going to see the comment sign and will skip over the whole thing. Comments are parts that you and the other programmers need to complete the code, but they are not important to the execution of the code, so your computer will just skip over them.

If you want to write out a code in Python, you simply need to use the # sign. Anything that comes after this will be ignored by the interpreter and you can even go over a few lines of the comment is that long. When you are done with what the comment needs to say, just hit return to start the rest of the code on another line below.

So all you will need to do in order to write a comment to your code is to add the # sign. It is going to look like this:

#This is an example of a comment

The interpreter will see this and just skip right over to the next command that you have. You and other programmers will be able to see the comment, which can be helpful for others who would like to use this code, but it will not interfere in the execution of your code.

Statements

Statements are an important part that you are able to add into your code. When you work on a code, you will be leaving expressions and statements inside in order to tell the computer what you want to show up. A statement is pretty much a unit of code that you will send over to the interpreter. The interpreter will take a look at the statement and then execute the command that you give to it. There are two types of statements that you can add into your code: print and assignment so far.

When you are writing out the code, you are able to write one or more statements at a time. For example, you can get started on a code and have it say a few different statements in the same spot. As long as it is still in the brackets and you are using the right rules with writing that part of the code, you can have as many statements as you would like.

When you add the statement or statements in to the code, the interpreter will get to work and execute what you want, as long as you have everything in place. The results of those statements, when done properly, will show up on the screen and you can make adjustments or changes as you wish. An example of how this works is:

x = 56

Name = John Doe

z = 10

print(x)

print(Name)

print(z)

When you send this over to the interpreter, the results that should show up on the screen are:

56

John Doe

10

It is as simple as that. Open up Python and give it a try to see how easy it is to just get a few things to show up in your interpreter.

Variables

Variables are going to help you to understand where your code is going to be stored on the computer. Variables are pretty much just spots on your computers' memory that are reserved for the different values of the code you are working on. When you start working on variables, you are basically reserving this specific spot in your memory for the code. Depending on the data type that you are using, the variable can automatically tell what memory space should be saved and it can also help determine what type of information you are able to store on this reserved memory.

Assigning a value to your variables

In order to get the variable to save to a particular part of your computer, you will need to assign a value to all of the variables. You can assign pretty much anything as a variable, but there are three main types that are often used. These three types include:

A string—this would be something like "Welcome to my Python program!" or another statement that you use.

Float—this would be like 3.14

Whole number—this one would be any of the whole numbers that you may use.

When using Python, you won't need to make a declaration in order to reserve memory space as this is something that can occur automatically once you put the value that you want inside the variable. To make sure that this happens automatically, you simply need to use the (=) so that your value knows where it should go.

Some examples of how this works include:

x = 12   *#this is an example of an integer assignment*

pi = 3.14 #this is an example of a floating point assignment

customer name = John Doe   #this is an example of a string assignment

If you would like to get these to come out in the program it is pretty simple to do. With Python 2 you can just write out the word print ahead of the statement, but Python 3 requires you to have the parentheses. Either way, it is pretty simple to get the information to come out. Let's take a look at how this will work below:

print(x)

print(pi)

print(customer name)

Based on the information listed above, when this is printed out, your interpreter is going to execute the results:

12

3.14

John Doe

Now is a good time to go onto your Python program and try writing this out. You will see that it is pretty simple to get something to show up on your screen. Mess around with this a bit to get the hang of how this program works and how little work it takes to get started on your own programming.

Doing multiple assignments

The examples that we gave above were for one assignment to each variable. But when working on Python, you can also add more to this. With multiple assignments, you are going to give one value to a few different variables. In order to complete this, you just need to add an equal sign between all of the parts and then the interpreter would know that all of them equal the same thing. The way that you would do this is:

a = b = c = 1

You do not need to write them all out together if you want. It is perfectly fine to separate them out if this makes more sense to you and the interpreter will still execute them in the same way. This means that it is just fine for you to write out the equation above as:

a = 1

b = 1

c = 1

Both of these would come up with the same results when you executed the program, the only difference is the way that you write it and that the first choice is a bit easier to read and takes up less space. But the choice is yours on which one you would like to use.

Data types that are considered standard in Python

There are a number of data types that you can work with when you are in Python. These can be used inside the code in order to define the different operations that you are allowed to do or in order to explain how they are stored in the memory. There are five main types of data that are common in Python including:

- Numbers

- Lists

- Strings

- Dictionary

- Tuples

Each of these are going to work a bit differently and will tell the interpreter how to execute the statements in a different way.

Numbers

The first one that we will look at are numbers. These are data types that will store the numerical values that you want to work with. They will turn into objects once you have had time to assign a new value to them. There are a few types of numericals that are common when using Python. The four types that you may use include:

- Int (signed integers)

- Float (floating point real values)

- Long (long integers)

- Complex (these would include complex numbers

When it comes to doing a long number, you are allowed to use both numbers and letters inside. For this reason, it is recommended that you use the uppercase L if you need it in the string. While the lowercase l is technically correct, it looks really similar to the 1, which could cause some issues when reading and executing the code. Most experts agree that you should just stick with the uppercase L to avoid confusion.

Strings

When it comes to using Python, strings are going to be the characters that are shown when you use quotation marks. All of the types of quotation marks are acceptable in Python, with the single and the double being the most common. You do need to keep consistency when doing this though. If you are using a double quote at the beginning of your string, you should end with the double string as well. This helps to keep the information together and will prevent an error coming up if the interpreter wasn't sure of what all goes together in the string.

You can also make some adjustments when you are printing the string. You don't always have to print off the whole string if you feel that this is too much or you want to make some variations to it. You are able to tell the program to just print off a part of the string, or even to repeat the string a few times. An example of some of the ways that you can manipulate the statement in order to execute the part of the string that you want includes:

str = 'Hi Python!'

print(str) #prints complete string

print(str[0])   #prints the first character of the string

print(str[2:5]) #prints characters starting from the 3rd to the 5th

print(str[2:])   #prints string starting from the 3rd character

print(str*2)   #prints the string two times

print(str+"Guys")   #prints concatenated string

In most cases, you will probably want to print out the whole string, but it is still good to know how to do the different options in case you want to mix something up a little bit!

Lists

Another thing that you are able to do with the Python program is work on lists. These are often considered really versatile data types on Python because you are able to contain a lot of different items in them, using commas ore the squared brackets to keep everything together. If you have worked with any of the C programs, you may have worked with a similar type of list before. The major difference between these is that you are allowed to add in several different types of data when working on Python while this is not allowed with the C language programs.

The values that you store in the list will need a slice operator and the [:] symbol in order to be accessed. With this type of option, the addition sign is going to be the concatenation operator and you will use the asterisk to show that you want everything to be repeated again. To see what this all means and how it looks, let's take a look at the following expression:

list = ['mainu', 'shainu', 86, 3.14, 50.2]

tinylist = [123, 'arun']

print)list) #prints complete list

print(list[0])   #prints the first element of the list

print(list[1:3]- #prints elements starting from the second element and going to the third

print(list [2:]) #prints all of the elements of the list starting with the 3rd element.

Print(tinylist*2)   #prints the list twice.

Print(list + tinylist) #prints the concatenated lists.

Tuples

A tuple is pretty similar to what you can do with a list, but it will have some different uses for the signs that are inside. The biggest difference that you will find is that when you are doing a list, you will use brackets and will have the choice of changing the size and the elements of your statements. With tuples, you will need to use parentheses and once you set in the information, you will not be able to change them. A good way to think about tuples is that they are a read only page that you can't make any changes to.

Other than the fact that you will not be able to make any changes to this program when you are using it, you will otherwise be able to use the tuple in a similar manner as you do with a list. This can make it a good option if you want to make a simple code that others won't be able to make changes to later on.

Dictionaries

Dictionaries are another important tool that you will be able to use when you are in the Python language. They are going to work similar to the hashes and the hash tables that you find in Perl and C# programming languages so if you have used these in the past, you will be familiar with the results.

When you are working in a dictionary, they are going to consist of value pairs that are key and while you can create the key to be pretty much anything in this language, they are often made to be numbers and strings to keep things easy. In most cases, when you are using the values, you will find that they are simply arbitrary objects in this language.

Let's take a quick look at some of the following codes to see how dictionaries will work in the Python language.

#dictionary stores key-value pair, later to be retrieved by the values with the keys

dict = {}

dict['mainu'] = "This is mainu"

dict[10] = 'This is number 10"

empdict = {'name': 'arun', 'code':23, 'dept': 'IT'}

print(dict['mainu']) #this will print the value for the 'mainu' key

print(dict[10])   #this will print the value for the 10 key

print(empdict)   #this will print the complete dictionary

print(empdict.keys())   #this will print out all of the keys

print(empdict.values())   #this will print all the values

Something that you should keep in mind when you are working with dictionary values is that you will have the values stored in the order that you sorted them in. the interpreter and memory will have no idea about ordering the elements and it will assume that you took the right steps to do this on your own. The elements will be unordered until you make the proper changes to fix this.

Operators and Operands

When you are working on a code in Python, you will notice that there are many symbols that will show up and they will often have more than one meaning based on the reason that you are using them and which basic function you want them to work for. It is a good idea to understand what they all mean so that you can write your code correctly.

In this section, we are going to look at operands and operators. The operator is mostly used to mean the various mathematical equations, such as multiplication and division as well as addition and subtraction. The value that comes out of the operator is going to be the operand. You will be able to use these different signs in order to have the interpreter figure out the value that you are looking for.

When you send the operators over to your interpreter, it is going to use the basic order of evaluation. Think back to math class and the rules that you were supposed to follow in order to come up with the right answer if there was a long equation with a lot of different signs in it. You would use the order of operations, which is the same as the order of evaluation on this system.

If your expression has two or more operators inside, you will need to make sure that everything is organized so that the interpreter is going to do it right. Python will use the PEMDAS system in order to go through and figure out the right answer. This stands for parenthesis, exponentiation, multiplication, division, addition, and subtraction. If you have more than one of each of these within the expression, the interpreter will go from left to right and will continue to compute until the right number comes out.

The modulus operator can be important as well. This operator is going to work with the integers and then will give you the remainder once your first operand has been divided by the second one. This can be a great way to get a few formulas done as the same time if needed.

Working with Python can be one of the simplest processes that you can do, as long as you understand what is going on and learn as you go. Remember that Python has made it really easy to work with the interpreter in order to try something out and see if it will work or not. This allows the beginner to work at their programming and to learn something new along the way with a bit of trial and error that won't drive them insane. And if you are ever unsure about doing it the right way or want to clarify something you have done, adding in a comment to the code can make all the difference.

Learning the Statements to Get Things Done

Python is basically going to react when you give it a command. Based on the command that you are giving it, you will get a specific response. So far some of the different commands we have worked on have been absolutes. This means that you will simply put in the numbers or the statement and then everything will pop up in the interpreter.

But there are times when you will want to make a code that doesn't work that way. Perhaps you want to have the statement only appear if certain things are true. Or maybe you want the possibility of having several different types of statements show up based on whether there is a true or false. This can get a bit more complicated, but chapter is going to look at some of the parts of "if" and "if…else" statements to show the different things that you are able to do with some of your codes.

For these statements, you are going to be working on an outcome of either rue or false. You will need to tell the program what actions you want it to do and what kinds of statements should be executed based on whether your outcome is true or false. One thing to remember is that when working in Python, if you have an answer that is zero or null, you are dealing with a false outcome and if you have an answer that comes out non-zero or non-null, you are dealing with a true outcome. Let's take a look at each one to get a better understanding of how these work:

- If statements—your if statement will have a Boolean expression. This is going to be followed by at least one statement, or more if you would like, that will only be executed if your answer matches up.

- If…else statements—this is another option we will discuss that allows you to have a few different options available. In the case of your "if" statement being correct, that first answer will show up on the program. But when the "if" statement is wrong, you can set it up so that a different set of statements shows up in the program.

- Nested if statements—it is possible to add either one or both of the above options inside of each other if you need it to.

An example of using the "if" statement would be:

```
age = 23

if (age == 23):

    print("The age is 23")

print("Have a good day!")
```

when this code comes through it is going to state:

The age is 23

Have a good day!

When you put in the "if" keyword to your code, you are telling the compiler that you are writing a control instruction and you are placing the conditions of the statement within the parentheses. If the conditions are true, you will have the code come out on the computer. But if the conditions are not met or are false, the interpreter is just going to completely ignore the statement that you have inside. For example, if the age had been 20, the interpreter would just ignore the whole code below and move on to your next command.

Now, in some cases you still want to have the interpreter give you a result, even if the conditions were not met. If someone is asking a question about whether the qualify for a promotion, you don't want the interpreter to just move on to something else and completely ignore them if their age it too young. This is when the "if…else" statements can come in handy.

With the "if…else" statement, you can have two statements, or sometimes more, show up based on the answer. Let's look at the example above. If the age does turn out to be 23, your original message can show up. But if the age is 20, you can use the "if…else" statement can provide another message, such as "you do not qualify, have a nice day!" so that the person using the program will at least get a message, rather than having nothing show up on the screen.

Figuring out when something is true or false in your statement can be the next challenge. You should learn a bit about the relational operators in order to get this to make some sense for you. These allow you to compare the values that you have to see if they are unequal, equal, or perhaps something else. Here is a good chart that will help you to understand what is going on with the operations so you can tell if your expression is true or false:

This expression	Is true if
X == y	X is equal to y
X != y	X is not equal to y
X < y	X is less than y
X > y	X is greater than y
X <= y	X is less than or equal to y
X >= y	X is greater than or equal to y

A good example of how this can work when you are just using an "if" statement includes:

age = int(input("Enter your age:"))

if (age <=18):

   print("You are not eligible for voting, try next election!")

print("Program ends")

This code will give you different outputs based on the age that is put in. If the person is younger than the age of 18, they will be given the notice that they are too young for voting and that they should try again later. Then the program will end. But if they enter a value that is older than 18, such as 25, the program is just going to end because they are older than the numbers that are shown there.

Now, you probably do not want to have your program just shut down after someone puts in a number that is over 18. This is when the "if...else' statements can come in handy. You could modify the code above to add in an else part that would print off some statement, such as "congratulations, you are able to vote this year!" rather than just leaving it blank. We will discuss these in more detail in the next section!

Working with "if…else" statements

We have talked about these a little bit so far, but let's take a look at some more with these and how they are going to make your whole code so much stronger and better than just using the if statements.

When you are working with just the "if' statements, you are a bit more limited in what you are able to do. You can put in a statement and other information that you want to have show up on the screen when the conditions are met, but if for some reason these conditions aren't met, the interpreter is just going to end the program and move on to something else. This can look bad for many programs because people may put in data to get some information and if your program just ends because their information doesn't add up to your conditions, it isn't going to bode well.

Luckily, the "If…else" statements are a great way for you to fix this. You are allowed to have two, and sometimes more, options based on what the user will input. For example, you can start out with an if statement. When this statement is a match, you will have the first statement that you write come up. But if the first statement is false, you can have a second statement show up. You can go down a few times doing this to really get some different options to show up because sometimes, a few things aren't going to match.

So whether or not the user is putting in the right numbers to match up or not, they will get an answer. For example, with the code that we had above about voting, if the user says that they are under 18, that "if" statement would show up. But if they say that they are older, such as 20, you could add in the "else" part of the statement and have something else show up as well. In order to get this to happen, you would simply add in an "else" clause rather than program end to keep the code going.

Elif statements:

Another thing that you are able to do with a statement is to bring in the elif statements. This will give you some options to check based on which of the expressions are true. This can help if you want to have a few options to pick from so that you can give out the right information based on the situation. The example that we are going to show later on allows the user to pick out the type of pizza that they want to order and gives a response based on their answers.

First, the syntax that you will use with the elif statements is:

if expression1:

statement(s)

elif expression2:

statement(s)

elif expression3:

statement(s)

else:

statement(s)

from here you will be able to add in the information that you want to the statement sections and then get the responses that you want based on what the user puts in. Let's expand out this syntax to get an idea of how you could use this in your program.

Print("Let's enjoy a Pizza! Ok, let's go inside Pizzahut!")

print("Waiter, Please select Pizza of your choice from the menu")

pizzachoice = int(input("Please enter your choice of Pizza:"))

if pizzachoice == 1:

   print('I want to enjoy a pizza napoletana')

elif pizzachoice == 2:

   print('I want to enjoy a pizza rustica')

elif pizzachoice == 3:

   print('I want to enjoy a pizza capricciosa')

else:

   print("Sorry, I do not want any of the listed pizza's, please bring a Coca Cola for me.")

The print lines are going to show you the statements that come up based on the number that the user inputs. So if they decide to go with number 2 for their pizza, the statement "I want to enjoy a pizza rustica" will show up on the screen for them to choose from. They will be able to make any of the choices that they want. Yes, this formula may seem like a lot of work, but it is actually a basic code that you can input and have a little fun with. Give it a try on your computer and see what Python pushes out for you when you put in different choices.

.

These "if" statements can provide you with so many more options when it comes to creating your own code. While the codes in the first chapter are just going to show up when you type them in, these ones require some information to be placed in first in order to give you the right answer. In the case of a simple "if" statement, if the conditions are not met, you are going to end up with the program shutting down.

But when you use the "if...else" and the elif options, you are able to really expand what your code and the program will be able to do. You can add as many else and elif statements as you want to each of them and change up the numbers as much as you want. Take some time to experiment with some of the options that you have and see how easy, and how much fun, this can be!

Working with Loop Statements

With the programs we have discussed so far in this guidebook, we are talking about those that are sequential or decision control instructions. With decision control, the calculations will be done in a fixed order and with the sequential, the interpreter would execute the instructions based on how the conditions turned up in the end. There are some limitations with this option because they were able to perform their actions just once. These actions would be done in the exact same way each time and they could only be done once unless you put the code back in again.

Of course, there are going to be times when you want to have your code work a bit more, perhaps have the option of looping the information over again. Loop statements can make this happen because they will allow you as the programmer to execute your statement or statements several times. You can often choose how many times you would like the statement to be re-executed depending on the type of loop statement that you choose. Any time that you would like to have your statement reappear in your program, rather than having it move on to another part of the code or end the program, you will need to create a loop statement within the code.

Loop statements do not need to be difficult, and Python allows you to use three different methods to place the loop statement within the code. The hard part is just figuring out which type of loop statement will work to make your code perfect. The methods that you can choose from in Python include:

Using a for loop

Nesting loop

A while loop

Each of these are going to work in a slightly different manner but they will all be useful depending on what you would like to do with your line of code.

The while loop

First we will take a look at the while loop. The while loop is a good place to start if you want your code to repeat or do the same actions a fixed number of times. If you are looking to keep the loop going for an indefinite amount of times, you will need to pick out another option, but the while look will help you to keep it going for a bit, maybe five or six times, before you send the interpreter over to another part of the code.

A good example of the while loop is calculating out interest. You may need to do this a few times in order to get the best results for the user, but if they have to go backwards in the program all the time, they could get frustrated. The following example will show how a while loop statement can work when calculating out simple interest:

#calculation of simple interest. Ask user to input principal, rate of interest, number of years.

counter = 1

while(counter <= 3):

principal = int(input("Enter the principal amount:"))

numberofyeras = int(input("Enter the number of years:"))

rateofinterest = float(input("Enter the rate of interest:"))

*simpleinterest = principal * numberofyears * rateofinterest/100*

print("Simple interest = %.2f" %simpleinterest)

#increase the counter by 1

counter = counter + 1

print("You have calculated simple interest for 3 time!")

For this loop statement, the user is able to input their simple interest numbers three times and when they are done, a nice message will come up on the screen. You can make this as simple or as complicated as you would like, perhaps adding in ten or twenty lines here for the user. The user can choose the numbers that they would like to add in for the interest and the interpreter will help them get the right numbers. They can also redo the program again, such as going back to the start, if they want to put in more numbers than three, or you can add more loops to this one to help out as well.

The "for" loop

For those who have used other programming languages, such as C and C++, the for loop may be a bit familiar. It works similar to what you will find with the while loop, and is the more traditional way to do things when working with these other languages. If you are planning on hooking Python up with one of the other programming languages, you may want to consider going with the for loop to prevent any issues.

With the for loop, the user is not able to define the condition that stops the loop. Python will have the same statement repeat in the order that you have placed them inside the statement. A good example of this is found below:

 # Measure some strings:

words = ['apple', 'mango', 'banana', 'orange']

for w in words:

print(w, len(w))

When you insert this into the code and let it go through the loop, the for fruit words (or whichever words you put into the code) are going to repeat in the exact same order that you write them. If you are writing the code and would like these to come out in a different order, you will need to turn them around in the syntax. The computer is not going to allow you to make changes to the looping order if you leave the syntax just like it is above.

If you would like the loop to just reiterate a certain sequence of numbers, using the range() function can be the best option for you. This will help you to generate a big list containing the different arithmetic progressions that you are allowed to use in Python and can make things easier.

Nested Loops

In addition to the two types of loops listed above, it is also possible to work on nested loops. These sound more complicated than they are but you are going to be impressed by all the things that you are able to do with them once you get started. A nested loop is pretty much a loop that is inside of another one. Both of these loops are going to keep going until the programs are completed.

A good example of doing this is to design a multiplication table inside of Python. This will show you how a few loops can get going in Python and how you are going to be able to create a whole bunch of information with just a few lines of code. Our multiplication code will go from 1 to 10.

#write a multiplication table from 1 to 10

For x in xrange(1, 11):

   For y in xrange(1, 11):

   *Print '%d = %d' % (x, y, x*x)*

When you got the output of this program, it is going to look similar to this:

1*1 = 1

1*2 = 2

1*3 = 3

1*4 = 4

1*5 = 5

This would continue going until you got all the way up to 1*10 = 2

Then it would move on to do the table by twos such as this:

2*1 =2

2*2 = 4

2*3 = 6

This would continue with all of the numbers until you reached 10*10 = 100. Loop at all of the things that you can get from such a simple amount of code. With the help of a looping statement, you simply need three lines of code (you could skip the comments if you wanted) and you have created a quite large table that could be helpful to others. This is the power that is behind Python and as you get more experience with the program (you should definitely take some time to try this one out to gain some confidence in all that you can do on Python), you are going to be amazed at how simple it is to do some basic things with this programming language.

Jon Stinkster

The Basics of Functions in Your Python Code

Another important thing that you will need to know how to do when working in Python is functions. Functions are just blocks of code that will be self-contained and will help you to complete the coherent task that you want done inside of the code. When you define your functions, you gain the power to specify the name of your function as well as which sequence the statements will be in. After all of this is done, it is easier to call this function up simply using it's name. In Python, you will be able to use two different types of functions based on what you would like the code to accomplish.

User defined functions

With a user defined function, you are going to be the one who defines any function that you plan to use. You will find that these kinds of functions have the same rules that are found with naming variables so this can make things easier to remember. You are alowed to use letters, both uppercase and lowercase, as well as numbers and characters, just make sure that you are not using a number as the first character of the name. Alos, make sure that you avoid using any of the keywords we discussed as the name of the function and avoid calling a variable and a function by the same name to avoid confusion.

After you write out the name in a function, you will note that there are parentheses. If your parentheses are empty, this particular function is not dealing with an argument. Next you will move down to the first line, known as the header, and the rest of the function is called the body. Make sure that your header has a colon at the end and place an indentatin for all the body to help the interpreter keep things in order and understand what you want to do.

If all of this sounds a bit confusing, don't worry. Here is a good example of a syntax that you can use when dealing with a user defined function:

def functionname(arg1, arg2, arg3):

   '''docstring of the function i.e., a brief introduction about the function"

   #code inside the function

   Return[value]

   #a function may not have any arguments or parameters like

   def functionname():

   #code inside the function

The function parameters work well with any of the other data types that you use in this language including int. float, tuple, dictionary, list, and user defined classes. Below are some descriptions of the different parts that are in the above syntax so you know what information to place in each part to make the code work for you.

The docstring function

One of the first indentations that you will notice is the docsring. In any function syntax, the docstring is going to be the first line present after your header. The documentation string, or docstring, will be used to explain what your function is going to do within the code. One thing to note is that the docstring is optional so if you don't put it in, your code will still work, but it is considered good practice to add it in for clarity. If you need the docstring to go over a few lines, add in the triple quotes so that the interpreter knows that everything should be together.

Return statement

No matter what kind of code you are writing, the function is going to provide a value. That is why the return statement is so important in this one. It is the exit function in this code and will go back to the exact place it was called from. The statement can have expressions in it that can be evaluated before it provides this value. In cases where you don't have the return statement or there aren't any expressions inside the statement, your return will simply be the None object.

Scope and lifetime variables

The lifetime and the scope variables are important parts of your functions code in Python. The scope variable is any part of the code that you are able to see and recognize while the code is running. Any of the parameters and variables that you add into the function won't be seen from the outside when someone is looking at the actual program.

A good example of this is opening up a program on your computer. A user is able to go through and see all the outputs that you have for the program and may even see a little icon on the computer if you designed that, for them to click on. But they are not going to be able to see the variables, the functions, and everything else that you wrote in order to get the code to work for them. The things that the user are able to see from the outside are called the scope.

But when it comes to the lifetime period, this is the time period that your variable will exist inside the memory. For most of the functions that you are working on, the lifetime is simply going to be for as long as this particular function executes. Once the function has returned a value, these values are destroyed so that you are allowed to place in different numbers and get new results.

A good example of this is with the interest loop that we did in a previous chapter. The user is allowed to put in the values that they want and get certain answers. But once they are done with that, the input and output will be done with their lifetime and will disappear. This allows the user to come back on and use a different set of numbers if they wish. It basically allows more than one user to go with the program and get the answers that they want.

Pass by reference

In Python, when you place a parameter into your code, this parameter is going to be passed by a reference. This basically means that you are going to have the parameter linked back to a specific place in the memory. If you go through the code and end up changing the parameters for some reason, you are also going to be making changes in the memory and this will be reflected through the calling function.

The flow of execution

The flow of execution in your functions is important. It is going to tell the program what you want done first in the code, what you want done second, what you want done third and so on. This is very important. Your interpreter is not going to read the code and then decipher what you want to happen first by logic or anything else. If you place something first in the code, that is the first thing that will come up when you run it.

When writing your code in Python, remember that the interpreter reads things from top to bottom. So you should place the first command that you want done as the first thing on the list. Think of this like your grocery list or step by step instructions. You will usually place the most important thing at the very top and then work your way down until everything is finished. This should be the same when writing out the flow of execution in Python.

Functions that are anonymous

In some cases, Python will allow the programmer to work with anonymous functions. Anonymous functions are basically ones that aren't bound by a name like the others are when they run. You will need to use the keyword "lambda" to tell the interpreter what kind of function this is.

There are only a few times when you will want to create an anonymous function. Usually these are just done when the function is only needed in the exact location it is created or when you consider the function as a throw away type. Your lambda function is going to work with the other functions map(), filter(), and reduce. The basic syntax that you can use with this is:

lambda argument_list: expression.

The map, filter, and reduce functions

If you are looking to work with anonymous functions, there are three types of functions that you should add into the code to make it come out the way that you would like. Map, reduce, and filter are the best ones to use with lambda because they will help to prevent linking within the code so that the function can remain anonymous.

The map function

You will use the map() function any time that you have a member inside of a list or inside of an iterable. This is one that you are allowed to use inside of the function, but for the most part you would like it in the argument part of the syntax above. It is often used to make a list in the system so any time that you need a list written out, the map() function can help.

The filter function

The filter function can also be a useful tool to have in your coding. The filter function is going to work in order to take elements out of a sequence when the function is true. Anything else that is in the function is ignored. The sequence should be either true or false for this one to work properly. This is a good shorthand version to work with because it will be able to pick out all the parts of the sequence that are true, even if there are some that are false. It is basically just going to go through the function and pick out any of the true statements based on the conditions that you apply. Any of the false points are not going to be caught by the filter function.

Reduce function

The reduce function is really unique among functions because of all the things that you can do with it. This one is going to work to take several values, you can have two or three and all the way up to hundreds, and then combine them to make just one value rather than having all the large lists around. Some of these sequences can be easy to accomplish while others will take time depending on how many values that you add in.

Let's take a look at an easy form of this. We will use the numbers, 2, 4, 6, and 8. When you use the reduce function, you are going to turn this list of numbers into just one value. To start, you would add together the 2 and the 4 to get 6. Then you would add the 6 and the 6 together to get 12. Then you can add together the 12 and the 8 to get 20. The 20 is the value of your reduce function. To show how this would look in syntax form, use the following:

from functools import reduce

 results = reduce((lambda x, y: x +y), [2, 4, 6, 8])

print(result)

List comprehension

While there are several ways that you are able to create lists when you are working in Python, list comprehension is one of the best. In addition, if the lambda function is getting a bit confusing for you, the list comprehension is a good way to get around it and avoid using this or some of the functions that we listed above. The list comprehension uses a simpler syntax and won't need as much work to accomplish. Take a look at the list comprehension syntax below to see how easy it can be:

*[expression-involving-loop-variable **for** loop-variable **in** sequence]*

Basically this is a way that you can avoid some of the complications that occur when using the other options so that you are able to get the lists that you want with your functions without all the hassle.

There is just so much that you are able to do when you bring functions into the mix. This chapter is meant to help you to learn the different tasks that are available with functions and to understand how to even get through some shortcuts if you need.

Simple Codes to Try When Learning Python

Congratulations! You have learned some of the basics that come with using Python as your programming language. We have taken the time to talk about the different things that you can do with Python in order to get your feet wet with the idea and even some of the benefits of choosing Python over another programming language.

In this chapter, we are going to take a look at some of the different codes that you can try out when you are first starting on Python. These are simple options for beginners, but can give you some experience with the things we have discussed in this guidebook while also having some fun. Let's take a look!

The magic 8 ball

All of us have used the magic 8 ball in our lives. You ask it a simple question and then can get a slew of answers as your results. Did you know that you can also do this same thing on your Python program? If you are interested in giving this a try, use the following code:

```
# Import the modules

import sys

import random


ans = True


while ans:

    question = raw_input("Ask the magic 8 ball a question: (press enter to quit)")
```

```
answers = random.randint(1,8)


if question == ""

    sys.exit()


elif answers ==1:

    print("It is certain")


elif answers == 2:

    print("Outlook good")


elif answers == 3:

print("You may rely on it")


elif answers == 4:

    print("Ask again later")


elif answers == 5:

    print("Concentrate and ask again")


elif answers == 6:

    print("Reply hazy, try again.")


elif answers == 7:

    print("My reply is no")


elif answers == 8:
```

print("My sources say no")

you can keep going on with this giving as many answers as you would like. The user should then be able to play the game and get different answers when they ask a question. It is a fun little game that can be a great way to practice using your new coding skills.

Rolling the dice

The next program that you should try out when working on Python is the rolling the dice game. This is another one that you will want to use your random module for because you want the answers to be random each time that the dice is rolled. You will need to set up two variable, the minimum and the maximum so that it doesn't pick out numbers that are not on the dice. So basically the minimum and the maximum are going to be 1 and 6.

This is also a good example of a loop function because you will want to set it up so that the user is able to roll the dice a few times. Here we will set it up so that the user can hit "yes" or "y" in order to roll the dice again. To get started, use this code to create your game:

Import random

min = 1

max = 6

roll_again = "yes"

while roll_again == "yes" or roll_again == "y":

print("Rolling the dice...")

print("The values are...")

print random.randint(min, max)

print random.randint(min, max)

roll_again = raw_input("Roll the dices again?)

Playing Hangman with Python

If you are a fan of the classic Hangman game, you can use Python in order to create this game while working on your coding skills. The word that you want the other person to guess will be represented by dashes that are lined up in a row. If the player does guess one of the letters inside of the word, the script will place it in the right spots. The player will be given 10 turns in order to guess the word in the example that we give below. You can always change some of the variables around to add more guesses if you would like. Here is the code that you need in order to create a great Hangman game for Python:

```
# importing the time module

importing time


#welcoming the user

Name = raw_input("What is your name?")


print("Hello, + name, "Time to play hangman!")


print("

"


#wait for 1 second

time.sleep(1)


print("Start guessing...")

time.sleep(.05)


#here we set the secret

word = "secret"
```

#creates a variable with an empty value

guesses = ' '

#determine the number of turns

turns = 10

#create a while loop

#check if the turns are more than zero

while turns > 0:

    #make a counter that starts with zero

    failed = 0

    #for every character in secret_word

    for car in word:

    #see if the character is in the players guess

    if char in guesses:

    #print then out the character

    print char,

    else

    # if not found, print a dash

    print "_",

```
# and increase the failed counter with one

failed += 1


#if failed is equal to zero


#print You Won

if failed == 0:

print("You Won")


#exit the script

      Break


print


# ask the user go guess a character

guess = raw_input("guess a character:")


#set the players guess to guesses

guesses += guess


# if the guess is not found in the secret word

if guess not in word:


#turns counter decreases with 1 (now 9)

turns -= 1


#print wrong
```

```
    print("Wrong")


# how many turns are left

    Print("You have," + turns, 'more guesses')


#if the turns are equal to zero

    if turns == 0


#print "You Loose"

    print("You Loose")
```

This one was a bit more complicated than some of the others, but it allows the user to play a whole game. The word can be automatically picked and will be random and the player gets a chance to mess around and play a fun little game. You can change how many times you would like to let them guess and other things to make the game yours so go ahead and place this into your program and see what happens!

Conclusion

Thank for making it through to the end of *Python: Learn the Easiest Program Coding for the Absolute Beginner*, let's hope it was informative and able to provide you with all of the tools you need to achieve your goals whatever it may be.

The next step is to get started writing your own codes using the Python language. We have spent some time taking a look at the various aspects of Python, from the main reasons that you should try out this language over another to how to download this free programming language to your computer and even how to write some simple codes in order o really get going on the program.

Python is such a great coding language because it has all the features that you will look for in a programming language, but with a much easier to understand format and the ability to experiment and see what happens when you try something new out. This guidebook is the resource that you need to get started with Python and to learn just what it takes to write some of your own code. Give some of these codes a try and see how they can work for you!

ABOUT THE AUTHOR

Jon Stinkster has spent his life shifting between Silicon Valley and Seattle. His childhood was surrounded by people in the computer industry. He doesn't remember a time when he wasn't on his computer. He found he had a inborn knack for teaching people of all ages how to do computer coding after teaching his 62 year old grandmother and his 12 year old brother, Sam (who he nicknamed Sticky) how to code. He followed his grandmother's suggestion to put his easy teaching style into his books. He enjoyed it so much he is planning to publish more books about the exciting world of computer programming for the new world which will see computers embedding in everything.

www.ingramcontent.com/pod-product-compliance
Lightning Source LLC
Chambersburg PA
CBHW080544060326
40690CB00022B/5221